INTO THE HEARTH

Into the Hearth

Poems

VOLUME 14

Wendy E. Slater

Into the Hearth

Wendy E. Slater books are available for order through Ingram Press Catalogues

Published by Traduka Publishing

publisher@traduka.com

ISBN 978-1-943512-00-3

BOOK DESIGN BY CAROLYN KASPER

COVER PHOTO BY WENDY E. SLATER

For the Truth

And

Path to it.

CONTENTS

What is a goodbye?
    Yellowed taxis, blackened limousines,
     SUVs with the charred
     Father, mother, or stranger
     Who carries us to the departure,
     The goodbye to what?

Leaving the moon,
      I welcome the sun,
      Always full, lighting
      The horizon before
        All appears,
      Not as an apparition
        Or vision,
      But commonality
        Of Truth.

It hurts
 That you haven't called
 Or found me to say goodbye.
 And yet you've taught
        Me
   Chalk to board
    Eye to eye
   Silence humming to my heart,
 Your absence
        Means neither
            Anything
            Nor
   Everything,
   And I will always
        Sing to your heart,
        And you mine.
 The uncertainty of not knowing
   Has folded back into
        The ocean
          Waves receding into the
            Other, arcing up and flatting down,
                Pulling under
       Only so edges
          Could be tasted and felt—
       Before we fold wildly
            Into the infinite
              Holding fishes, ecosystems,
            And the electric eel, sulphur
            Springs, hidden entrances,
                All in our taste and our tongue.

I miss you, miss you, you
I long for and yet you are
In the heart. The unknown is
Knowing I must let the tide
Flow in and out, neither
Harnessing nor harboring,
As we float and be
Under stars, constellations
Held by moon and gravity
   When it is meant to be
      Neither forced nor
         Held but free and wild
            And blue and green.

I see the goodbyes
   Held at bay,
Spilling onto cement walks
When the levee breaks after
   Idling a little too long
     In random cars
   Lighting up the landing
    Pattern, and what
   Stories are held in the hesitant:
    Reluctant windows closed and folded into
    Stilled movement and conversation,
   What tale would the valise
    Scream if all that
  Was tightly wound and stuffed
  Was flipped open in a moment,
  In this instant, or that
  Moment, and who am I
     To them? If they
    Notice?

Drivel drives me mad
   And dulled to
Be in its presence,
  Which is all too present
  In this aeroport,
  Departures, closing the gap
  With strangers and known
  Entities with random
  Muted nothingness.
   If we were all
    Silent for one
   Random moment in unison,
  Would the tethered ropes
    Dissolve and true
  Nothingness breathe into
    As an always
  Such that there was no
  Holding in within the inhale
  And fear of loss
    With the exhale?

Random nothingness and it's all begun,
    Into the hearth, into the
    Belly of passion, not as
    An explosion, but as
    Magnetic stillness
       As the North Star
       Or meteorite in motion
    Eye finds without sight
    And scope
       In that instant, a fleeting part
    Of an arc, and it seems
    So immense, so auspiciously
       Random as it
       Comes into the core.

I may need to change seats,
　　Those that surround,
　At a distance, are not random,
　Too close in utter idleness,
　Not like a car warming up,
　　But dizzy despair
　　Of not having touched
　　　Their souls or
　　　　Any souls in their
　　　　Driven moment
　　Of names, devices, histories
　　　Laced together of routine,
　　Following the same
　　　　Highway day in and day out,
　　Polite, mundane, politics of
　　　Superficial fabric
　　　That tears the skin
　　　　With its voice.

Could this late plane
    Arrive
  So I can find solace
    In the loud roar
  Of engines such that
   Voice cannot come to my ear—
And the raging silence will
    Bring peace
      In a way to me?

Is into the hearth
    Going to be kindled
    Into the flame
    Before I reach the
    Land of jasmine
        Gold and incense
        Breathing into my pores
            And out because
            The gate has opened?

What's in a hello?
    Singular depth and density
    Of inspiration, rootedness
    And more than coincidence,
        Such that I understand
        Like breath in my vision
          On a cold frost morn,
      How and why the constellations
          Join above and in my heart
        Which cannot wait,
          As it is all now,
            Divine inspiration
          Of seeming random
              Moments.

It is rare wisdom appears
             Out of nowhere
          Like cold breath
            Blowing larger than afield
            From a doorway.

I have arrived
  To stray dogs
  With welcoming smiles
    No cows
    But flavor, textures and smells
    Humid fog
  And thick with the
      Rooster's call,
      I wonder if I will sleep.

The greatest present
  To give myself
 Wrapped in this yellow bow
    And I just opened
    The receiving,
   Receptivity of all,
 And wonder at the fear,
    Shrapnel of old
     Has kept me apart,
 And one by one tonight
      The bayonets will be plucked
      Like wild daisies in the
        Field
    Such that wind and seed
      Can blow out and through me.

There is a deep ebbing,
    Loneliness in this place,
      The motherland
   Is neither in time nor space,
     But my imagination
    Brings bars and rules,
       And freedom of spirit
       Cannot be grounded
       Here I am
       Always in retreat.
And the clarity of focus
    Is not giving a fuck
      If I smoke or not
      When pesticides are spewed in
        My space,
      There is a randomness
    That is contrary
    And contradictory to my heart.
I will come to do what I need to
      On this mission,
   And then set sail for the
      Adventure
     Of always being true
       And in my pulse.

Into the hearth
  Is knowing that the flame
  Is rampant and spontaneous
    Vivid and contagious
And it does not abide
    By dictate, doctrine,
      Or constraint.

I had to come far out of the self
  To ground into the knowing:
I will not and cannot abide
  In another's domain
By rules that make domination
    Even from the sincerest of heart
    Can hold a false precept—
    For me,
The randomness of these dictates
    Elicits fear and imposes the decree
    To conform
  When insecticide is sprayed,
      It spews into my
    Ventricles, and I will not hold and pump an indoctrination
      As my blood or essence, but know
    The possibility of all the fabrics
      Textures before
        The bleaching from this external imposition,
    And so with these
      Grains, I will
    Do my mission
        And depart,
      For the core's truth
      Of beer, cigarettes, yoga
  Laughter, trains and freedom
        To fly away
      Always in my heart,
      Always in my time,
      Always in my pulse
        Of the flame.

There is no
    Beer to warm the heart
    Relax the mind
      Nor smoke in the lungs.
And it's not as if I don't know
      What to do with solitude—
    I really wonder if it's that
      They don't.

In the constraint,
 The passion, the hearth flame,
 Goes aside.
Two weeks and I will be moved on to
 A new adventure with sleep.
To be holed away from the sacred terrain
  Of
 Life and festivities and freedom
  Is not my style
  At all.

I get it now
　　As a red light
　　　　Not just in front
　　But boxed in by
　　　　Was never mine
　　　　　　Nor meant for me,
　　　　　　But tyranny
　　　　Comes in forms, color
　　　　　　And the boot
　　　　　With the boxing glove,
　　　And this is about me
　　　　And the glowing dance
　　Of lights expanding out
　　　　Like radiance,
　　　　　　Smoke of incense
　　　　To call me home and
　　　　Then you
　As this Northern light
　　　Will no longer
　　　Step aside from the imagined.

　　I am here.

The delicacy
    Of these sounds:
A train, lizards in the bush,
    Distant religious music
        Loud enough for me
        To chant with,
    Celebration of voices
        Rising up into the sky
        Simplicity with sitar
        Climbing with the moon,
          Quarter crescent,
    A lute and the stars
        All become you
        Me, us.

There are stories,
 Fabrics, footprints
Of families, lovers, man,
 Wife, children,
And I long to be
 In their company,
 Their kitchen,
Eating rice, smiling,
 Laughing, playing
 With the cherubs,
Being truthful in our
 Hearts that speak
 The same bold
 Tender gospel
Of now, acceptance,
 And spontaneous vividness—
We do not need to
 Understand the different languages,
But sitting in peace
 Amongst the dappled tethers
Of truth as one
 Is what I would
 Like,
A fire in the drum,
 A fortress made
 From silent acceptance
 Of as it is.

Austerity
  Has a badge
  And roots in domination.
There is neither room
  Nor space
  Aside from the one
    Or the collective us
    In despair of a loss
      Of individuality.

It's a 2:00 A.M.
    Silence with the howling
        Of the pack
  And I am not the target of stars,
      Neither in their gravity
        Nor collapse as the meteorite
        Trebles across the matrix,
    A bird calls
      In seeming randomness
        From one to another
          And again
    I shift the gaze to the right
      And notice a palm
        Leaf
    In grace
      Never perceived
      Before,
The rage is coming up to go
    So that peace can
        Truly fold in,
    As the bull's-eye folds up
      To recede.

To recede at 2:00 A.M.
As the pack
Yaps and howls,
I wonder of their story line
With mine
Baying and yapping
To sing the song in freedom
Of distress.

To sing the song of
   Freedom, not in despair
   I need to know, to believe
   A dependency cannot and will not
      Be cultivated
   To hold the seeds of betrayal
      Distress and loneliness.

The disturbance of sleep
   Will not endure
   An echo
     Of what was
   A breathing in and out
     As the ashes on the pyre
     Do not set sail
     But dissolve into
     This salted ocean
      Of love,
     Of the heart,
   It is me recycled in
     One breath, two breaths
    Inhale, exhale, pause, sigh,
       Tears of joy and calm.

The rooster's announcement
  Of dawn
 Is fighting
  With the crow's
   Declaration of the day
 And neither realize
    The prayer song from afar
 Is drowning out their chorus
   Together
  It resonates.

Chiming, plucking,
  And swooning
 With the sweeping of grace
  Across the sky
 And moon to bed
   And stars to rest
    From eyesight
 As the sun's always
   In the heart and eye
   Breathing love
    Into this territory
 Of seedlings: flowers arc
    And the stems swoon.

A banana leaf
  Can and will offer all the
   Shade needed
  And shadow of dark
    Will not reach into
    Ever

Again it shall be a place
To rest and sleep
And contemplate.

The grace
Of the vast expanse
Of the universe of the heart
Of compassion, kindness
And sweet tenderness,
Nectar flows ripe
Yolks of free love,
Unknown cages
Bent away
And freedom reigns.

In peace
And the bird song
Of the yet not known,
Unnamed,
But to me, is the sweet cackle
With the chip, chip, chip
Next to my ear, as the
Lute of love,
And the enjoyment
Roars loudly
With laughter,
Twittle, twittle, twittle
Is the note
Of the others, together
And apart
By tree species and nests
Of different heights and depths
And making,

They call this place home
To me
Safely
It is the lotus.

Not unfolding
But full
Blooms, not singular,
But a bouquet
Of scented nectar
Softness that must
Be outlined and touched
Again and again
And again
To raise the question
Of why it was never known
And kept inflamed
Such that heart
Swelled and the body,
Too,
In a disability
Of love
Of not being able
To root and breathe
And take in the
Rains, unless the
Monsoons threatened
To uproot.

And only
Then would the holding
Take deeper meaning
Such that resilience was

Survival, an ability
For trespass to cease,
Such that nectar and seeding,
Height and vigor
Were rare pilgrimages
Gripping onto life
Rather than sweet
Natural evolution of day
Into night
And such whether here
Or there
Or anywhere.

Instead of genetic resistance,
Like the hybrid seed
To withstand drought,
Blight or decay
In the face of natural
Shifts rather
A resistance to Man's
Invasion of taste, smell, texture, pollution
And greed,
And now resilience of love, home,
Self, and vivid completeness
Of the moment
Shines forth
In any and all
Aspects of
The external imbalance
Caused by avarice
That I have no need
Nor no longer in peril
Of freezing out alone

As the only
Anemone bred
To withstand the
Desert, a Sahara,
All me.

And now I see
I was out of orbit,
A caldera in the Stygian
Undiscovered craters of the moon,
Contained, dark and so cold,
Or
Jupiter or Mars
Where I would never
Be seen nor found
Until an eon or moment
Produced space craft
To locate
This jasmine ecstasy,
Finally discovered
Locked away, so resistant
It caged me in past
Our orbit, our gravity,
As from afar, I blended
In and anear.

A bizarre misnomer,
An anomaly of biology, evolution,
And genetics that
I would be the great discovery,
But they would not know
The story I tell
Of resistance, the strength of

Survival, of steps so large
    I could walk from here
Past the moon
    In a drunken stumble,
Do a twirl, and have an
    Espresso in Saturn's ring
    And still not be home
    As resistance, the survival,
    Keeps you alive,
    But dissociatively
    Separate.

And now
I sow those seeds of resistance
    In a bath
Of sandalwood, lavender, rose oil
    And rooster calls, dawn's break,
The tweet-a-cheet-cheet-cheet
    And the lizard's skitter
Such that deep grieving
    Is transmuted in a glance
To the Truth, the breath I now
    Share not as a loss
    Of identity, or evolutionary
Give and take, but as laughter
    At resilience of Truth,
    I have let it go,
And finally, finally
    Come home
As my own
Nectar and stem
    Waits for it to fly in and

        Taste and add
        That to the fruit
    of life,
            We all share.

But in this taste and sharing
    Nothing, absolutely nothing, the Absolute nothingness,
        Is taken, neither hoarded
            Nor mimicked, no longer.
    And in this giving and receiving of
            The bee onto my landing pad,
        Petal, stamen, and pistil,
        Nothing, absolutely nothing, is
        Invaded upon, nor trespassed,
            Nor imprinted
        As a destined trace of the caged
        Treachery or betrayal,
        There is no capture.

My breath is simply the Universe's
            Arc through me; I have
    Touched this breath, this O_2,
                CO_2, and the H in H_2O,
        And so have you,
The rooster, with its twit a twit chitchat,
The myrtle, even the cow, and the
        Water buffalo,
It all cycles through and out,
            It is not ours,
        But the preciousness of life
        Of the Universe.

Some dwell
        In shadows and others exposed
        Too long, and in my breath
I will neither dilute nor transcend for
        Another, but know the truth.
I leave no trace, no cosmic
Imprint, and only purity
        Arrives in my heart
        And leaves
        Only, only, only
        Our universe
And we are so small
        And the breath so large
Such that sky and stars
        Are simply beyond our
                Imagination of vastness—

But know,
        This is in the heart
        And out,
The matrix is not just in us.
        It is our skin, eyes, breath, and touch,
We are one,
        Always,
        In grace of the infinite,
Such that to one atom in my exhaled
        Breath from beginning to end
Can not imagine the vastness of all this
    Letting go nor its place in relation
        Nor how it fits or belongs or began
And the confusion that must set in
        When it drops to the ground
        Or the rooster breathes it in
                For another strange voyage

And never could this atom imagine
      The lungs or all that was part
      Of the cosmic imprint.

The electron ceases to be
      When it is in stillness
And in the big bang of love
      It knows, without magnetic pull or push,
That it is everywhere
      All once,
      And the journey and story is never told
        But always known.

And the path is breaking the bond
        To cohesion such that
Responsibility for the self, lacking blame,
        Is truth and kindness spilling
        Forth such that
Hatred and greed cannot bond
        And created compounds
        Bases and acids
        Break apart
So the golden Truth of always
        Without judgment
Can simply be. So simply be,
        And into the hearth of purification
          Of the heart we will be
            Residents of this,
            Always.

What is gravity of love?
  If it is out of this orbit,
      Then is it gravityless?
      Ridiculous?
What is duplicity of love?
    Is it the body's hearth
        With wood and no
          Embers to rekindle
Such that one must steal
    Fire from another
          To carry an essence,
        A thievery of love,
        That does not belong?
I know so,
        Such that self-responsibility
        Starts now,
    Find your own matches and gather
          Your wood and tend to
          It lovingly.
If you do not know and were
          Never taught to kindle
          Your own, then
        Now ask,
        Ask yourself, ask for direction,
        Ask for conscience, ask
        Ask, ask, dialogue
          With truth of matter—
Nothing is better than everything
        That accumulates as
          Stolen goods

In a bank account,
Rich, greedy and
Illiterate to the
Universal laws of our
Universe, ours.

What is the archangel of love?
　　It is the universe holding
　The seed of truth
　　In the palm, its palm, our palm
　Opened wide, neither fear nor danger
　Of trespass, no hesitancy
　　　Of abandonment, no longing
　For more, as it has always been,
　　It will always be
　Ripened, awake
　We seem
　　To dream in a moment's blink
　　And lucidly let go,
　And the remembrance is always
　　　There.

The salted ocean
　Folded into one wave
　　　And the next, ebbing
　And flowing, it makes little,
　No difference, the pulse
　　　Continues in body and out,
　The journey is to tenderly
　　Awaken the self
　　And then the other
　To knowing we are the water,
　　We are always
　And the cause and effect
　　　Will cease, not as stagnation,
　　　But as a disengagement

Of force of mass and acceleration
Of destruction, of the holding on
To a false sense of destiny.

The path is known only when
One ceases to exert the force,
Speed, to gain the arbitrary distance
On a grid that upon examination
Holds nothing but Karma's
Maze, a labyrinth
Of twists and turns,
Shadows and obstacles
Of not being nor having enough
Even to know the
Truth of ecstasy of
Being purposeful, self-responsible,
Untethered compassion like the butterfly
Folding in
To the song of morning's prayer
Or night moth, so large for the eyes,
Resting in the shade,
Here, just for a day
To be discovered and seen
If the eye doesn't
Try to find,
And then to notice it is gone
The next dawn.

There is neither resolute despair
Of abandonment nor rejection,
Nor violence, but a notice
Of its graceful presence
In that cove

Sheltered so close to the heart,
Free and without
Agenda, but purpose of nectar,
Food for one or the other,
And being home within the
Self and of course,
The tribal language
Of sweet silence of word,
There is not purposeless
Chitter chatter nor neglect
But resonance, resilience
Of intent.

This instant,
    Which is not the now,
  Is full of aggression,
     Snarled tigers in chains
    Only want to roam free
     But held high in view
      For its beauty and prize
      On the cager's terms
     Of pretty cat, meow, meow, meow,
When all it wants to do is roar,
      Be proud of its stripes
    And nature
     Even if that transcends
  To a bullet in the hide
    And a head on the mantle,
For there is no difference
    Between the arrogance
      Hidden behind seeming
        Benevolence of protection
     And the seeming randomness
    Of the kill.
One is breathing, but not free
   Of spirit, in the pen
  Limitations way too small
    For the natural instinct,
  But pride of the cager's
    Swells at sparing the target
  To be saved
    On his mantle in his field
    Of pocked daisies.
The other is simply the other.

To be witnessed
    Is to be in grace,
  And to be watched
    Is like walking through
A minefield of eyes
    Not blinking
As each twitter and twitch
    Is marked, noted
To be randomly forgotten
    When one stepped
    Away from this lost paradise
    Which Milton could have
        Written backwards.

I get it. Totally.
  In entirety
 Like the full moon beaming
   From my head,
  I have failed as
 A non-smoking, yoga, retreatee,
 Vegetarian diet
  With practically
 Crippling colored waters
   Of herbs
  That do me no good.
 I know I belong with a beer,
   An occasional smoke,
 Freedom to choose
    Who I love and what I love
   When for me, I love
  To leave and will in 5 days,
   First class if I have to
 As a celebration of my
  Success of knowing
   Where I belong and who I am.

Five days seems like an eternity,
　　　　But freedom knowing I will leave,
　　　And this is wrong
　　　　　Not as right and wrong
　　　But wrong like a dead
　　　　　Dull bell gong going off
　　　In muted groans.
Freedom, grace, and knowing of self
　　　　Is who I am
　　　And where I belong
　　　　In the hearth
　　　　　Of the home always
　　And no longer seeking it outside
　　　The self.
I long for excursions of Truth
　　　　And spontaneity, heart to heart,
　　Ear to eye, not dominance
　　　And false ideas of knowledge
　　　　Because of a degree
　　　　Of haughtiness, to need to
　　　　　Be in control, well
　　Let your control flippin' fly
　　　Cause I'm out of here
　　　In 5 days—
　　Even if I have to walk or
　　　Find a camel.

If I dove up and
   Through the arched and veined
   Dome of ivy trellised
    Over the crown
  Would I reach through to you
  And would I find
    Myself at home
     In stars, of the ocean
      And in the forest
       Of love
     Clasped as 2 hands
      In a voyage
       Of the unknown
      And trust in the
      Celebration of
      Surrendering all the feminine
     Into your masculine
Dowry of treasures unfolding
    As sacred nectar
   Cultivates and ripens
   To flower in the always,
     Wisdom to be
      Held
     As we disrobe
      Into nothingness?

What exactly
   Is nothingness
  When two bodies, archetypes
     Of love and mystery
     Of flamed feminine
       Rising in the steady
       Ravished masculine
     Merge into an infinite oneness
         Always
          Nothing
           Neither empty nor present
    As we inhale and exhale
       As all the constellations
        In the night sky
   Or
     Every forest bird
       At dawn
       In symphony and grace?

It is you and I
    Blue and green
      Sky and ocean
        Painting the canvas
     Of our merging, family, life,
     I can only hope,
       Only hope.

The leaves I thought
    Were talking to me
  But really now
    It's the wind
  Speaking in soft nuances
      Of jasmine, sandalwood,
      And the palm
    Of love to be, love that was
        And that love that always
          Is
      With memories and scents
        Outlines and tracings
        Arcs and bows.

How could you,
    No, how could I,
    No, how??
  The vague recollection
     Of sweetness
    Spent and wasted
     Burnt into a shadow,
     Ashes
   That I bow to
     And blow
     Away.

In blowing it away,
    Sweeping the ash pyre,
I claim the hearth
      As mine
      And know that I can be
      Loved
      As a woman
         Fruiting and bearing
         Vibrant and blazing
         Vivid and subtle
         Bold and stunning
  In glares, passion, artistry
         Or a smile
       And the hand sweeping
        Across the breast
        Again and catching
      Breath as the dense
  Cookie cutter imprint
        Of aping, coercion,
       Blindness and gaping smiles
        Of treachery
         Do not
      Hold me nor my future
        Ocean eyes come to my
         Hand and heart
         And my bed
         And home
        And arms
         Ours.

How blue is blue
    When resonating
  With bold love that can not
        Hide nor want to
  From gentle tender love
        For me as your world?
Blue is so blue
        That I swim freely
          In warm
          Caribbean waters or Mexico
          Stunned at the grace, elegance
            And surprise.
Blue is so blue
        That the sky
          Eats me up
            Alive again.
Blue is so blue
        That a hearth could only ever
          Be a home
          In your arms.

Your arms,
   You,
  And my hope
    That you have discovered the time,
    The courage I thought you were
      Lacking
   May simply have been
      Wounded battered heart
        And soul
     Withered parched
        Desiccated
    Such that veins of love
       Raining
    Scared me of both
       The drought and the
        Tsunami
        All over again.

The geckos
  Make their home
  On my temporary wall
Every night the same
  Distance between
Like stars or planets
  From afar
Never seeming to shift
  In location, thought
  Or dialogue.
Tail to tail they hold
  The complex
  Geometry in the nothingness
  Between them
The stuccoed wall
  Echoing and sheltering.

Do they hear the birds and
  Feel the wind like I do?
Does Mars or Neptune
  Or Polaris
Sense my tide flowing
  In and out
Waiting, patiently waiting
  For you
  And our graced
  Complex geometry
To meet as arcs, spirals,
  Amorphic shapes
  Of blue and green?
  Holding space

Day in and out
  Like these geckos
Subtle and profound is truly
  A mystery.

I'd really like to let go of this feeling
        Of ugliness,
    Worse yet that somebody
    Stole my beauty.
    I see swollen face and nose
        Thick neck
    And bloated belly,
        It all makes me feel
        So unwomanly,
But not because it is
        But because the deception
            And treachery, violation beyond
        Description that took place
            In full view
                With a drop of this
                In my food,
            A drop of that in my teacup.
Steroid poisoning or varnish for
            Breakfast would make anyone
            Look this way. But I don't
            Have the story to tell
                    And
            So I bloated to show the abuse
                    Which I have now left behind
And in my hearth and home
            There shall be beauty and joy
                Freedom and movement
                Love and love.

Movement,
    Although just the scraping
    Of leaves, a history,
       Against wood: my bone,
  Still startles
   Like prey in the brush
     On edge of life and death
           Black and white
           Night and dawn,
    Or the stillest moment
        Before the opening of
    The potential,
  Caught in a breath
   Stilled
    To expect the predator,
But it's only the hum of nature,
   All that is
      Dancing in joy against
      My skin,
     Only that,
  And I no longer hold
    The breath,
   I do still momentarily
    As a way to reassure
     Before the exhale.

It is bland light
   This morn
    Before the fog disperses
    And the eye sees
    Clearly, as if for the first time,
      With first sight of the
        True self.

What if we were born
    Into ourselves
  In the predawn light
    Neither able to see the self
    Nor the forest clearly,
      Neither leaf nor ground nor stem
        Evident
  Nor the faint song of gecko in the bush
      weaving into
The loud crow of the rooster
    And the random tweetles of a bird
    Letting us all know the day
      Will arrive?
And we did not have vocabulary
      For hope and longing and despair
      Nor conjure ideas
        Of separation, isolation, loss
      For the stars to hold
And asteroids to whisper
      From one orbit to the next,
Would we fundamentally remember
      Not to forget
      Not to let fear
        Into the toes and hearts
And feel nothing more than
      Radiant beauty
        Of the moment
      Being all
    There ever was and will be
    Such that stillness was not stagnant
      Fear of holding breath, on edge

For the next moment
Until we learn to thread
It all into some insane
Story line of hierarchy and domination
Rather than the complete sense and knowing
We all beat and pulse
Exhale and inhale
In concert without randomness
Of purpose and content
Such that direction is not found
By navigating with the stars
But letting the heart be, Simply
Be, and that means
Eyes wide open
Knowing
The earth breathes, the sky
And ivy, too—
The superimposition of thought
As to where we belong
Is not to substantiate
Like math equations
Or logic of geometric patterns
Our musing stance
By strategy or astrological denominations
And calculations—
To the stars, sky, and moon,
We are nothing, simply nothing—
Does Saturn have charts and blazes
To define its existence
By one more birth or death
Or exhale and inhale?

There is some master breath analyzer
On Neptune
Calculating its planet orbit turn and
Revelation
Based on how and when
We will all breathe as one,
And then, and only then,
Will Great Mystery
Be revealed to us.

I love
  I truly love
    My mornings here
    As they are my own
And the view of dark to predawn
    To the awakened moment
    And the expansion
Is like being the lotus seed
      Stem, flower, and the pond
      Birds, grass, and the tiger
All at once awakened, unfolded
      Revealed that we are
      All and nothing
    But exquisiteness of
      Absolute sameness
    Whispers, laps, ripples, licking
      Tickled petals by the dew
      Drying off for vigor
    All in plain view
      Of your golden blue eye.

Rain is not a weeping
   Nor is leaf to ground a sadness,
  It is simple sharing
   To fill joy and fruiting
      And rebirth
     Into the next
     As day into dusk
      Night into dawn
      Sun into moon
      Love into tenderness
     And my arms into yours.

I awoke
  To the realization
That I slept with the door
    Wide open
Heart with no fear
  A relaxation into self,
      In the home and of
    The hearth.

W ENDY
O NCE
W ONDERFUL

I S

A T
M Y

A nnouncement

P oetic
O mni
E legance
T otally

The veil, the drapery of the night,
　　Has lifted from the eyes
　Sheers of dappled light
　　　Random moons
　　　And the planet of my
　　　　Heart
　Is free from the contrast
　　　Of light to dark
　　As song, a symphony
　　　Is sung
　　　And always singing.

Flame is not as evident
        In day
    But smoke is in full sight,
By night
    Fire is evident as
Vibrancy of colors
        That sing the song
Of flowering petals
            From heart, womb
                And eyes
        I speak in song.

A random voice over
    The crowded room
   Will claim authority
When the mimic
      Is
    Like clown
  In a business suit,
Authority comes in subtle forms
    Of mesmerized light
   Stolen from other's treasures
    To seek
     Only glory
   Masked as self-help—
    It's all part of
    The evolution,
But the power is still
     Being taken,
   The flame and fire
    Doused
    Only to be accessed
When they link up to
    The cult leader,
     The weakest one
   That grows large
   And taller
With big high heels
     And the microphone
    Of mind speak.
If we pulled back all the robes
    From the oaf,

The grand wizard of Oz
Dwarfed by truth
Would wriggle out
Like the worm
Full of casings
Debris and detritus of
Hidden longings
And agenda
For nothing but followers
Like a mad parade in
King Of Hearts
Duplicity created the walls
Rather than
Unlocking the door of the heart,
That harbors
Others in the fortress
To gain strength,
And of course money, so
Much money of poverty.

Poverty of spirit
    Is not elective.
   A lack of funds
    To feed the soul
   Is a complex situation
Partnered in self neglect.
    If we are not taught
   To examine and question
Drought, monsoons, and even the blizzard,
      Rage is in full sight
      Of the dawn
      Always there
      Of ecstatic
      Merging of jasmine flowers
      Dripping love
      And dew
      And nectar
      Of the ultimate
      As vividness,
        Always.

A random noise
   Has such random meaning
     To such random eyes, ears, taste, smell, and touch
But your touch is precise and open,
    Yet, continents separate us,
And in time and space
   I smell your sweet ecstasy
   And feel your open palm and fingers
       Mapping my terrain:
        Our world,
   And to know your fingers
     On my lips,
       Tracing our love and my taste
   Is like arching back
     In warm blue calm sheltered waters
  As you wave over me
     To taste and shield
     From sun and
   I am nothing and everything
     At once, always,
     In the knowing of you.

What would it be like,
        Truly, in truth,
    If we folded like smoke
    Spiraling up into nothingness,
    Disappearing from sight,
            But touching, seeing, tasting, smelling, hearing
    Everything at once?
            Not as a mixed sumptuous bowl of soup
                With elegance and flavor
                    Enough for any palate,
    But as a symphony blended
                In rapture, an orchestrated
    Ensemble of love, divinity, and ecstasy
                Such that trumpet and violin
                    Blare with truth
                And vehemently resonate
                    Life
    And one may listen to the
                Delicate strings in concentration,
    But it would not be a celebration
                With the whole troop of players,
                    Listen, listen, listen
                And you will hear
    And then sight, sound, and touch and
                Smell will awake
                Like nothing
                    Nothing at all
                Else it be hidden
                    From view.
                This is yours, open to it,
                    Dance, celebrate and love,

Be the audience, the field,
    The sitar and the banjo,
    The conductor,
    Even the janitor and the
    Neighbor with the window
    Wide open who cannot
      Come out to see, but
     Only hear,
By dark and in the light,
     Awaken,
    To the fire in the hearth,
      Make music and be.

A random noise,
 A seemingly random racket,
 Is not arbitrary,
The train, to me, sings the song
 Of India, freedom,
 Chai, histories to tell
 And generations to come
  And arrive,
To another the train
 Is barbed wire, smothering
 Cattle cars of people, bodies
 On bodies, and history
 Has always
 Taken it away.

I trust
    I trust in the unfolding of knowledge
        Of known breath
    In the palm of the hand
        No longer upside down
          And ringed
          Nor boxed
        But winged and soaring.

We come curled in the cocoon
    Folded back in the banana
      Or palm leaf
    Luminescent colors and
      Magnificent heart song.
We only need to bend and
    Flex and examine
    The unfolding
  As it comes with grace, ease
    And honesty
Even in the pained truth
    Of separation and seeming longing.
Rather many wait in despair
    For the other to unfold
    Not as an intrinsic
    Geometric dance of
  Movement, bells, and dance
    But as a holler and wail
    Of helpless stamina
      Of gasping and gulping
  Waiting to latch into
    Rather than be set free.
    Fly.

The dawn comes,
The song has arrived,
Familiar scents move in and around
And my breath
Expands outwards
And I am gracefully wedded
To the earth
Its soils and textures
Of clay, rain, crunched
Leaves and even
The snake
And bee sting,
It is all so complex
Simple as the laughter
Out of my belly—
Or the rooster dancing and claiming
His terrain,
Which is my heart, too.
One cannot demand or bequeath the absolute
In or to another
With direction
Like a road map
From India to the heart
Or the coastal highway to Oregon,
The truth of the universe unfolding
Can only be taught
By painting, words, artistry of
Soul that heals the
Wounds, brings forth
Gently the questions
And transmutes the holding.

The absolute is simply what it is
Not in direction
And with compass and insight,
It is always pointing in,
Directly in,
To unfold,
Non-dependent and
With kind compassion
That can without
Old magnetic holdings
Be the slap on the ass
Stinging and red
But without clinging and agenda,
Stay to the path,
The journey of unfolding.

I arrive with ample time,
   And in the absence of chaos,
I am vivid, vibrant
    Stilled and full
  Of knowing, sweet chits
  With the birds of love
That grace the arc above
    The head and heart
And clear the space for
   Divinity to sample
    My taste
   And remind me
It is all here,
    Always
    Whole.

If it's always whole and complete,
    And expansive beyond
     Expansion, depth that
Cannot define depth as
      The mind, in abstraction
Or logic, arrests the heart
       At times, and ceases
     To comprehend the alchemy
       Of magic in a touch
       Or breath. Did you know
      The absolute Truth
       Touched you yesterday?
     And now,
       Always
        In grace
      Fall into and
       Veils will be swept
       Away.

What is a hello?
  One must let go of the good-bye
    First and know
  It is only then that
    The true hello, kiss of absolute love
    On the eyelids, soul of absolute
    Tender wrathful knowing
    Can unfold for there is
      No hello or good-bye
        As in shut doors,
      Hung up phone, hugs not to be
        Seen again, as it
      Is always the dawn
        Folding into the day
      And day surrendering to dusk
      And night coming out
          To dance
      In the hearth,
          In the flame.

I do know the despair
   Of feeling the link
   To the Absolute
   Has been absolutely forgotten
   And brought me to my knees
 And so weary
   I have remembered and do remember
   The link is not a chain
       Not a thing,
      There can be no attachment.
      It's all within.

Touching the despair of abandonment,
    I have thought I could never
    Be loved with a man,
And in that forgetting,
     Like a blink
    Or nap in the hammock
      With foot dangling in the dirt,
Truth has resided in me always,
      And when I awoke
    And still awaken
     From the drugged torpor
I have wondered,
      Where and how could I
        Hold these thoughts,
     Like some precious treasure
      Of absolute false wealth?

If I could be anywhere for a
      Moment,
   Well, it was the last moment,
   'Cause this moment I want to be with you,
I would be at home in the hearth and heart
     With a beautiful pint or two of the absolute
       Nectar, fresh draft,
        Or bottled,
      And maybe a smoke, too,
       And look up to
     The stars and just be
       In my crisp dawn
        Ecstatic
       In my own little way.

I have not forgotten the Taste,
How could I?
At home it's night, and I know
Just for a moment
A glass of divine Pinot Noir or Cabernet
With a beautiful dinner
Of the heart from you,
And ecstasy would reign,
The hearth is on flame,
Vivid, ecstatic,
Graced
And simply wanting
The comforts of
Home
Which are here, always,
If I could taste
You, I have me,
Now, us.

The golden hue
    On the coconut leaf
   Tells me the dawn
     Has passed,
    And what does it tell you?
I do long, at times, and I do
    Not disguise or mask
     That truth,
    But the grace is settling
      Me so
     Back into my heart
      And soul,
     Such that longing for you,
      Is losing
      Its flavor and taste,
        To be outside of the self
      Where cacophony resides.
Perhaps, the paths will not
    Cross and I must be
     In grace with that.

If we were at home
        With the children
    I would be making the stew
        To fill our bellies,
And awaken the taste and touch and smell
            And sight
        While I had a pint
            Of our love
        And baked the bread
            Of our seedings,
        And tended the hearth
            Of the sacred flame
                In us all,
            Because we would be one.
                We are.

Is the longing my awareness
  Of the transcendence?
 The lack of fear to paralyze
   Is now an awakened catalyst.
  The same could be said
    For anger, sadness
   And the ecstatic laughter.
But when the other will not touch
   The grace
   Of the universe's breath
  Through logic and binding fear,
 Then where's the point?
   And again it all
  Recedes and ebbs like a giant
    Meteorite of letting go dropped in the ocean
    Of our love
  And it all goes on from
    There
   To wait and see and be
    But I will always love you,
     How could I not?
    Always.

And this love
   That is always
   Makes me know
   That being in the now
     Is being in the open expanse
      Always
    Such when the grace of you
     Walks near
      I will see and know
       And so will you,
         Won't you?
       Said the sun to the moon.

It dawned on me
That we have been in relationship
For years, epochs, eons
For the purpose of burning off external
Karma, dissolving fear,
Finding our voice, truth, pulse
Such that in true union,
It will be purity into purity,
As you breathe ecstasy
Into
By touch, sight, sound,
And the food
From the hearth.
I love you always.
No matter what
Unfolds
You have brought me
Back to my
Hearth safely and without
Rules or dependency,
But a simple pointing out of
Instruction. You are
Divine and I want to
Taste your lips on my skin
And touch your flame
With my breath.

Touching flame with the breath,
    Is simply like bringing more O_2 to fire,
    And when in concert,
   The Tantric ecstatic of all
      Builds and builds and builds
        Until we are free
          From structure.
         I love you.

Hello, hello,
　　Where are you?
　When longing comes into
　　　So does fear.
　　And to be in the heart from afar,
　　　　Always near, present,
　　Always the Trust to radiate
　　　　From here to eternity
　　　Such that blaze
　　　　Transcends it all,
　　From hearth to hearth
　　　I am wedded bliss
　　And await the touch—

Which will happen so naturally
　　　And always dependably resilient
　　Like waves against the edges of sand
　Or cliff, such that the journey,
　The huge journey, the only one,
　　Has begun a long time ago,
　And will come into being like
　　　The breath or tide, without effort
　　Or calculation,
　　　　I love you, sweet dear one.